SECRETS OF A WORLD UNTOLD

SECRETS OF A WORLD UNTOLD

POEMS AND SPIRITUAL REFLECTIONS

Troy Dennie

iUniverse, Inc.
Bloomington

Secrets of a World Untold
Poems and Spiritual Reflections

iUniverse books may be ordered through booksellers or by contacting:

iUniverse
1663 Liberty Drive
Bloomington, IN 47403
www.iuniverse.com
1-800-Authors (1-800-288-4677)

ISBN: 978-1-4620-0535-2 (sc)
ISBN: 978-1-4620-0536-9 (ebk)

Printed in the United States of America

iUniverse rev. date: 04/07/2011

People ask me why I write.

It is a question that does not allude to an easy answer. Writing is such a lovely medium for expressing one's thoughts and enabling access to a wide variety in audience. I enjoy writing to a degree, I am not crazy about it to be real.

The message, love, hopes, dreams and stories I spread to my people is what I really feel. Can't promise that the topics will always be non offensive, but my word; they will all be reflective, collective and open to perception. Truth will be delivered from my being to your reality, knowing that our *truths* are relative to our understanding, agreeance, and acceptance of our world; I believe the real **truth** cannot be denied and relies very little on relativity.

The message is love, and it's not mine either, it is God's. God's love transpires all, creating beautiful rivers and lakes, mountains, the sun, the moon, babies, opportunities, painters, parents, memories, inventions, athletes, all constant reflections of God's omnipotent power, grace and love. I have used internal messages of love received from the humility of God's nature through lessons in scripture of biblical and modern contexts. Through respectful observation of Islam, Christianity, Raja Yoga and Taoism I have been able to learn life lessons and truths that exist universally. My spiritual path has led me to a place of peace and placed me in a position to help many, and I am doing the work I was meant to do with peace, integrity, respect, equality and love.

This is a lot to sum up in a nutshell or epilogue for this matter, so check it out for yourself. You might want to go somewhere quiet, get a warm drink, put some therapeutic songs on, light some candles or incense and vibe out. I live by these words : love for all, conscious of one.

Bless

CHAPTER ONE
-
OPEN YOUR EYES

IN A LAND.....IN MY MIND

In a land where people can be observed at will and degraded based on financial reservations

In a time where masses can be influenced by digital messages and anagrams

In a place where my thoughts travel with the clouds, my words fly to the sky and reincarnate as condensation, with this mental levitation there is only elation

In a body that can train for the Olympics or sculpt the most beautiful of pieces, perhaps articulate vast notions and therapeutic motions.

In an atmosphere that allows us to adapt to our extremity of environments, compose bodily functions and ailments, disperse kindness and sickness, develop mentality and personality based on the individual's anatomy biologically and psychologically.

In the mode of the abstract and the mood of the jazzy and neo central soul, the quota for authenticity and remedy for social stresses

In my mind where I refocus, realign yet never rewind,
I allow love to transmit, consider this the eternal
happiness transcripts, metaphysical spiritual transit,
through and out your brain to your internal domain,
in the age of greatness and span of man, grace of
woman and a historic time

All this can flow from the depth of my mind

Yet,

Temporarily I dwell

In a land where ...

NOT AFRAID TO BE REAL

Not afraid 2 be real
I can't control how others feel nor do I strive for a mass appeal
I'm tired of people accepting oppression and capitalism, monotony and consumerism
Some make reference to the heat in the kitchen yet 80% of folk in mental prison
If each person helped a stranger there would be less danger
World wars one and two were systematically orchestrated, Illuminati infiltrated
Hepatitis, aids, malaria, genocides delegated
Health and information manipulated
Truth and history or herstory fragmented
Religious origins sacred and recently obliterated
They put a price on the education they suggest determines whether you 'make it'
Freedom of speech was given to me in Heaven before my Earth birth
So I keep it real and inform my folks of the evils and their corrupt appeal
Told us about good and evil so several chose the worst
Unaware of the curse
I put love first, this encompasses God, fam, my soul; all
This young man and his plan to re-align the stars
Let you know we're closer than they show
Cats win thirty million dollars over here while some can't feed their kids
Celebrities on the tube, yet around the globe there are homeless, global warming
-hunger-poverty, oppression, hell's resemblance
Lets talk about dividends
Don't be mad at the past
Learn for your own knowledge and strength, not to enhance your cash
No one wants to listen, they'd rather complacency and bitching; soul connection
missing
Prophets all dead or in jail
Corrupt will lie to our kids to increase their sales
Doesn't matter if we appear dark or pale, muscular or frail, they put humans on a
scale, play their game designed to fail
Play God's game and in peace you shall dwell
Freedom is what they will **try** and steal
Not afraid to be real

Modern Revolutionary

Modern revolutionary
Intricate visionary
Aligned with the only son of virgin Mary
Infinite being living in a world of temporary
I'm bodacious in my manner since slavery was hereditary
Love me hate me fear me
I know you'll hear me
Regularly rhyme relativity and relational celestial philosophies
Simplicity and solidarity
I can save you from ambiguous obscurity
Words and verbnosis beyond a dictionary
Modern revolutionary

<u>Synopsis</u>
This is really how I think, I acknowledge the universe and solar system; finding great relevance and wonder in their beauty and science. In my eyes the soul/spirit of Christ is in me, and although peace is my mission I realize that my strength cannot be compromised. "Bodacious in my manner since slavery was hereditary" one hundred and fifty years ago I could not say this, 2500 years ago the world was not ready for a black leader; I must not let my strength be compromised, I spread my voice in this unique time and life span of mine. I am seen as complex, however my understanding and approach to life adds simplicity -simplicity and solidarity. Look deeper than the words on the page, see the concepts behind the words, ask yourself why can't you be a modern revolutionary? Or better yet, ask yourself if you are; the answer will be there right in front of you.

<u>the irony</u>

The irony of life is what provides the ultimate lesson and humour. If you refer to humour even in looney tunes, Wile E. Coyote on a determined path to capture the roadrunner, flying through obstacles, creating new means to gain leverage on his prey, yet despite all his attempts the wit and quickness of the roadrunner always proves more efficient; the irony.

The irony in our language is that most of us do not even understand the words we use and think we know. A lot of words we use to associate success, importance, and value are only ideas. For example great, cool, smart, articulate, athletic, responsible, handsome, sexy, etc. All such words-adjectives only DESCRIBE or attribute the truth, the person or thing, all persons or things are of exceptional power. Rather than look at the words we use to describe people or objects, let us realize that without our words such would still be present. Without the word tree, human, love, life, greatness, purity, even without our understanding of such words; the essence of their description and of that they are describing would still stand. The irony

Imagine man and woman uniting in what we call holy matrimony, a lifetime commitment to the 'love' of your life, in a world where people try to love with possession and expectations, leading to confusion and misery, divorce and dishonesty, or a fifty percent success-attrition (all on how you see it) rate of 'successful' marriages; the irony

Somehow people feel they should dissect, disrespect, classify, judge, and discriminate on others, who are like them, yet for some reason like : ethnicity, age, gender, sexual orientation, race, educational, social status, reputation they are mistreated; and all would like to be treated fairly- laugh out loud- the irony

All of those tough, turbulent, stressful, distracting, painful, apparently horrible times that lay behind us and we feel caused us so much grief are soooo in the past. Check it out, regardless of all the reasons you and myself believed that those obstacles were the worst thing at the *moment* they are all over now; shoot - the irony

I live my life in the light of love, help others, keep it real and although my messages are sincere, I hear and see several who insert xmas for Christmas, who acknowledge things which are imminent yet claim their difficulty, swear to or about others, and ignore the simplistic beauty within and among us, this beautiful universe. The same people who will be crying profusely at funerals asking why, how come, its not fair and Lord give me strength or denying a heavenly omnipotent presence, only to continue living a life of misery, prolonged hope and fallacy before returning to the light and magnificent grace of love and the one; the irony

A lot will read this, a lot will be aware, many have been on earth, all will pass temporarily only to be born a new, babies speak in hidden gifted transcripts, love will prosper and hate only divides, we are all beings of light, impossible to dwell in darkness 4ever, I have sooo much power to coincide with my purity, as we all do; THE IRONY

It would appear easier for people to believe they do not have the answers but others do, it would also appear favourable for several to ignore me than to accept me as a beacon of light and a saviour to myself and possibly others, here for love and happiness to be spread, the reflection of eternity and infinite peace;
the irony

Remember the thing that happened to you last week, then you shook your head almost in disbelief or subsequent humour, and said to yourself "now that's ironic!" do you?

                        THE IRONY

Twinkle Twinkle

Twinkle twinkle in the sky, up so high, perils of those who want to fly, nightly bright, free from flight, will it be tonight that the few in power surrender to the forces of equality, not if the fighters of equality are being unequivocally quiet, not suggesting a riot but please do not just watch and sit by as people avoid turmoil yet still lose their life, advocate or die, how you livin'? or bye, make love to the money mistakenly or dabble in so called illegal trades to eradicate the stunning effects of grades, oh stop it behave, don't divulge in the fact you're ancestors were slaves, Chinese built our railroads yet they ask for little, aboriginals as we now refer to were here long before the terms immigration existed, blacks vs. white still exploits of **the** racist, reverse racism is the same as holy atheism, non existent, reminiscent of the Phoenix without it's wings, Michael Jackson that don't sing, Kobe without rings, Tut minus the king, before the bling it was simple, when paths appear wrinkled, merely point above and hear twinkle twinkle...

I AM

I am Earth

I am life

I am love

I am the force that moves the ground

I am the warmth of a volcano

I am the rush of excitement

I am the echo of the shadows

I am the breeze of the brilliant

I am the sunset and sunrise

I am the lunar phase and the moon

I am the butterfly and the cocoon

I am because Rene Descartes told me : I think so therefore I am

I am all that I wanna be and more than I say I am

I am the wind between the trees

I am the truth

I am the message and the messenger

I am real

I am free from judgment

I am eternal, infinite, mortal and immortal

I am the renaissance

I am the present and I was the now

I am not who you thought I was but I am who you see

I am TJD

I am a product of the eighties

I am in my state of karma

I am the chooser of my own path

I am responsible for my happiness and my glory

I am categorically cool

I am me so I accept you for you, even though you are me and I am you

I am the dopest to ever be me,
shoot

I am the only me

I am

IN MY DREAMS

I dozed off early last night, fell into the <u>dream world</u>.

When we close our eyes, we envision all possibilities in our dreams...

In my dreams I see my grandpa, we play dominoes and the time we share is unparalleled. I use multiple strategies to evade his dominance in dominoes, but we all know how that goes. I asked my grandpa how he played with such ease, he said you tell me, this is your dream.

In my dreams the lottery doesn't exist, but shoot neither does poverty. Fields of children playing endlessly with no worries in the world, adults walking to work and greeting the commute neighbors, the news is filled with uplifting information and positive feedback, injuries are reversed, divorces ain't necessary and marriage is not mandated. Sometimes I miss my boy Josh, know how he loved him some ice cream, so we both have two scoops in my dreams.

In my dreams we are all united, smiling, loving, in a perpetual rhythm of passion and appreciation

In my dreams, I can fly, you can glide, and he can soar, she can levitate, and we can reach the clouds

In my dreams I see PAC, Michael Jackson, <u>Princess Di</u>, Gandhi, I even see Hitler and he ain't on that violent tip anymore, shoot not in my dreams . . .

In my dreams we all take five minutes a day to center ourselves by regulating our breathing and meditating on positive thoughts

There really isn't anything or anyone I have not done or seen, no need for phones or tv; only smiles and laughter everywhere I see' in my dreams .

WHAT IF

what if the two you call mom and dad were more like friends?

is that where it's at now, then shoot, where will it end?

what if you knew money could never equal happiness, and it's worth couldn't be transpired past death, would we still seek overwhelming wealth?

what if pac could see what they were saying to big, and notorious heard what they told shakur, would they be here?

would things be like before?

possibly no east coast west coast war?

what if it was 1546, and Tim Horton's didn't exist, you could openly spank your kids, terms like global warming held no relevance, and we never were told to jump by two kids named Chris?

what if we had wings and could see how amazing this planet really is, could we still be angry at one another, would you see the harmonized significance of words like sister or brother?

what if when you read this joint, you be thinking it's hella on point?

what if religions differ, can my thoughts still anoint?

what if the first kiss was the last love and the last kiss was the first love?

what if we could see the future and you knew how it was all gonna go down, could you alter the future's present by diffusing the right now?

what if I'm just cruising but cats tell me to slow down, what if where they're at is behind my past and my moment is beyond their sights, could that explain why I vibe out to myself at night?

what if I started this at six thirty four and ended by six fifty six?

what if the answer to your question of is that the truth, was; it is what it is?

yooo, what if?

SOCIAL PARAMETERS

donating to charities knowing damn well it won't reach the intended destination

ask myself if <u>technology</u> unites or increases segregation?

footsteps of the young to the beat of the <u>nomadic</u> drum, do you hear the faint whisper of the <u>homeless</u>?

is it wrong for the addict to crave rum and if so how can one not help but feel hopeless?
maybe less questions and more didactic ways, less rendering and more experiencing, eliminate the lust and illuminate the love.

take a few steps into your backyard, stroll down to the extent of your neighborhood, emerge from your surroundings to some new findings, tip toe to the <u>Savannah</u> or valleys of the East, venture to the mountains off the coast

envision yourself as a wolf, how would you talk to folks?

you can buy the best drugs at shoppers and pollution pollutes our lungs by the hour, plus for the grave we paying a whole lot for some pretty <u>flowers</u>,

most people who get paid well walk around looking sour, maybe <u>consumerism</u> induced their greed and thus their <u>soul</u> was devoured,

sometimes its more than literal; like these cats are dirty and in dire need of a shower, maybe I'm doing like Kanye and trippin' off the power

exposing you to the scenic, evading the morally anaemic, detailing axioms so real that you don't have to believe it, they tell us there is a jackpot even though we never see it

from the time you born your path seems preordained and the inspired route seems strange,
they assume if you ain't educated then your car must be stolen,
young girls long for affection prelude to their legs open,
labelled him King James because we presumed he was chosen,
the persistent tap into the stocks looking for an omen,
read this and your soul is vibed out on that neo tip even if only for the moment,
what if its 2010 because time was once frozen?
if the moon and sun had a race who would win?

I wonder if the clouds are kin <u>folk</u> with the wind
if our language was comprised of many, then maybe we should reconsider the term *sin*

boats to <u>sports</u> coats, illegal soliciting to mourners reminiscing trafficking of all types, extradition of one who has freedoms and rights

poverty and malnourishment, resilience and encouragement

some things seem to worsen while others never get old

as always

love peace and soul

Immense Love & Solidarity

I have developed a rare distinction; it has to do with my internal vision.
I know of truths and live in a way that cannot be found or supported in society's make up
for success.
It would appear that my love for all is essentially appropriate, folks suggesting and displacing
my steelo, I only ask you to look beyond the physical and embrace my soul.
Most aspire, me, I'm on my holy tip, when folks condemn me I sense their loneliness.
It's all to the good, for some strange reason my realness makes them fear me; immense
love and
solidarity.

Aftermath

Psychedelic melodies teleport through my lobes
mind in control, in tune with thy soul
more than one thinks *we* 'know'
beyond the globe
past the thought of time, several have failed to realize the obvious, those
who pocket it look for where the profit is, all souls are eternal tell me who
the prophet is
simply rhetorical
metaphoric is most of my rhetoric, this is the truth's chicken soup; all can
afford it
lets support it
remorse present, regret absent,
suddenly hovering above the plains, welcomed by the clouds and soaring in
an element of peace, detached from emotional pain or personal gain
as the beat in my heart perpetuates to synchronized vibrations I am
awakened internally
this piece is expressed in the form of words as the manifestation of
thoughts and actions, rather than create a reaction I converse with the
infinite faction,
align my steps down the keys of life on my habitual piano,
rhythm of oxygen, dance of the wind, birds in motion as they sing,
this is the scar, an imprint on _____ soul,
conceptual holy water, take a bath, not so much one life to live as I have no
beginning I have no last
associated axioms and confessions of love
verbal jazz
spiritual hypnosis
this is the aftermath!

Now Is The Moment

Now is the moment, my decisions made in pretence since it Is, and must be I who chose it at the moment which has now elapsed.

Feel the skip of the beat to the breeze of the trees in sequence with the sea, I can hear the ease and I see the peace, I know the real, I speak in vague dialects and perplexing notions to disrupt the poison being dispersed to those unaware, each second is another to smile, ain't nobody know how soon will be a long while, so let's laugh and groove to the beat of the new, I think of the endless possibilities and immense discrepancies that serenade such scintillating melodies.

Modules for success are also methods for mediocrity, I refuse to accept the idea or fact limits can hold me back, I am acknowledging the essence of life mentally, emotionally, physically along with spiritually, and metaphysically understanding the complex simplicity of atoms, rearrange the perceived random and observe the evident patterns.

Tones and volumes of knowledge, flows and symphonies mixed with vintage memories, watch me coral the enigmatic personalities of divine souls on all sides of trees.

Captivate yourself, motivation lies within, embrace what's up more than just the time and seconds, I ain't here to condemn nor condone, we are all kings and queens, it is time to take thy thrown, would you relish in it if you were shown it, could you capture the evildoer if you were the culprit?

I'm down with the now and there, I am the when and where, life is naturally me so whom shall I fear?
...
Pause let's wait a minute, take a few, just embrace it, appreciation in the present, dig the vibe and dabble in the verbnosis - I said now is the moment!

CHAPTER TWO
-
THE ?S WITHIN THE ANSWERS

Sexual endeavours

Is it the lust or the feel of comfort we ensue and enthral ourselves in and with out,

do the strokes of tenderness and the intent to arouse come from the source, are all innuendos love of some sort, or is it to you that the sex is just what you expect, orgasm here, fling there, whose next? Perplexed at the case of the ex, urban daters call it a flex,

does tension commence with sex? Or do you make love, like those of us who are love, breathe love and only see love, so conceptually to sexually we only make love, is that too much to think of, no question mark, intercourse til bodies are numb and hearts are submerged, mate til union, spiritual retribution

INTROSPECTIVE: SEXUAL ENDEAVOURS

My name is Emma Fitzgerald.
Troy and I met when we were 11 years old in elementary school, and ever since we have been family. Sexual Endeavours is a piece written that is different from the others but carries the same meaning, **LOVE.**

One evening in particular, Troy and I arranged for our usual coffee and catch up date.
I always know when Troy has been writing because the instant I see him his eyes have an illuminating glow and his eager hands are on his blackberry. By this time I anticipate the "Emz take in this note." Troy began to read me one of his notes, it suddenly dawned on me that he had wrote on every topic except "spirituality" and its correlation with "sex." I suggested it to Troy and within minutes "Sexual Endeavours" evolved.

This piece speaks of **Love** through no age or ethnicity, instead it speaks of **Love** in a context as we see it, an "act" but more profoundly a feeling we may not truly know like we think we do. It gives readers a chance to identify with themselves outside of the social norm, not only for one present second but into a renewable future.

PuRpOsE

I don't expect you to like me

It is not important whether you understand me

I am not here to administer anything to you except for myself

Myself in totality is the truth, undenied and uncompromised

Subject to my own rules and volition

Purpose derived from within

Intent is to live life fully by my means

Purpose

From Wikipedia, the free encyclopedia

Purpose is a result, end, mean, aim, or goal of an action intentionally undertaken[1], or of an object being brought into use or existence, whether or not the purpose was a primary or secondary effect. It is possible that an intentional act may have multiple purposes, only one of which is a primary intention while the remainder are secondary intentions. For example, the introduction of a gene into a species of rice may have the primary intention of providing resistance to disease and a secondary intention of reducing nutritional value. The diminished nutritional value, though perhaps regrettable, would be a secondary intention in that it is a known effect willingly accepted
With love comes hate, or so it seems, what about all those who fall between the seams?

Deep thoughts on a higher plane,

Truths that may not be able to be explained but believe it or not they were preordained
What is life to you and why do you choose to live it?

Do you stay awake and alive because you feel you have to, or is there a specific reason and purpose for such prolonging?

Perhaps a perpetual path of pursuit for happiness, or rather an immediate recognition of our innate ability to create happiness

If what I am saying to you seems irrational, or illogical then there is no medium or format available that would allow ME to prove such to YOU

However I know it is not my purpose to prove such things to you, it is merely my karma to provoke minds and evoke thought with freedom
The rest is up to you, but you already knew that

So let the little stay less and the more manifest to the best
Allow the easy in your life to transmit grace to the difficult, while the dark forces at work preach the occult

Let me take you down some different roads, after that you decide where to go

It ain't always about being fast or slow, it has more to do with knowing why you are really trying to get to where you want to go

Doing things that have never been formulated because my thoughts are cosmically correlated

If today is my last, it has been a blast, and most of my life is in the past, so I am immensely rich without the notion of cash

KISS THE YOUTH, RESPECT THE SENIORS

teach me how to fly and soar above the clouds, escaping the perils of stress and fatigue, eluding the worries of death and sorrow, dwelling in the celestial balance

allow me to hold you, keep you warm in time of winter, uphold you for your views and love, disregard the notion of you as a sinner

get with the new and interrupt the old, understand the now and process the then, reorganize the future and be the architect and viewer, help the ones who are lost so that you are the user of language and no longer the abuser of love

kiss the youth, respect the seniors, nourish the teens, harvest the young adults, obliterate all such labels and embrace all, reflect on where you went wrong, learn to see how we stay right,

kick it with this modern day philosophy, Troy Plato Jermaine Aristotle Socrates, lineage from the west indies, deeper down the line the coasts of Africa was home to ancestors of mine, prior to those times we were relishing in the current middle east, we were in the light before and I intend to increase the peace

dream, think, believe, know, want, see, ask, trust , be, know, wonder, hypothesize, strategize, *human* **beings** open your eyes!

BASEMENT CONTEMPLATION

Have to learn when the water treads too steadily and one is not ready, this is when things can get messy.
Imagine what it would be like if each girl growing up in the former soviet union realized their affiliation with the higher cultivation, could it possibly be a different vision, of man and woman, capitalism to communism, societal prison?

When a lady has to test multiple men to determine who is her baby father, someone to love them, truth is if dude doesn't know he's the dad then he probably gave her more than she could handle, sex is only a trophy upon a mantel- for most men; and woman are left with outstretched arms and empty hands.

The hungry walk to the bodega and corner store, get some chips, a Philly, and whatever else change can provide, hustling white when shit gets rocky we are told to take it in stride, when the cops out brothas hide, sista's hold it down and say less than they know while knowing more than they show, no dad, no college fund, no after school programs, this is just the tale of a few hundreds of thousands a' millions with enough debt to build mountains, poverty and tragedy is sadly astounding in cities over the globe too many to identify via counting

Haiti and Pakistan still struggling despite five billion in donations, these bastards withheld the help we provided and allowed the people of travesty and their issues to be subsided, my eyes are weld up with passion for the blind, being strong for them so no crying, crying ain't soft though, trying to be hard over crying is merely lying.

I make you think and if not I'm gonna make your ass think harder.

These are just my thoughts and ventilations,
cognitive condensation,
humanitarian meditation,
rhetorical medication.
Let the world reach elation, eleven, fourteen, twenty ten, my basement contemplation

DOPE NOSTALOGY

WASN'T IT I WHO WAS SUPPOSED TO BE KING OR IS IT ME WHO WAS DEPRIVED MY TONGUE AND GIVEN THE LANGUAGE OF THE ENGLISH? DON'T WANT TO LIVE LAVISH, CHOOSE NOT TO SIT AND LANGUISH, YET I CAN SEE THEM CONFLICTED WITH MY CONVICTIONS OF CLARITY AND COGNITIVE EMISSIONS, I ADVISE THAT MY TELEPATHIC PERMISSIONS ARE METHODICAL REVISIONS TO THIS SYSTEM THAT HAS US UTTERLY CONDITIONED. I KNOW THE JEWS OF THE TRUE AND THE <u>ARABIC</u> WHO SPEAK HEBREW AS WELL AS THE FOLLOWERS OF <u>GOD</u> BEFORE CHRISTIANITY CAME TO, SO LET'S UNITE THE MUSLIM AND THE JEWS, CONNECT THE SIKHS AND HINDUS, EMBRACE THE BUDDHIST AND ATHEIST. DON'T CONDEMN THE RACIST THAT MERELY PUTS US IN THE SAME PLACE, THE PREFACE OF THIS SURGE TO RESHAPE THE EARTH AND HUMAN'S FATE IS THE CORRELATION WITH MY ESSENCE AND THE ORIGINAL DATE.

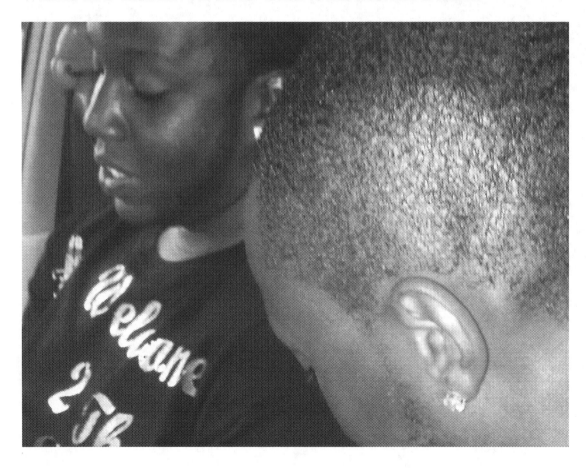

I'M KICKIN' IT WITH T, MY RIGHT HAND, EMPEROR AND KING, ROYALTY AND BLISS, ABOVE THE GROUND TWO YOUNG MEN WHO WERE ONCE KIDS, MULTI TASKING AND GIVING WITH LITTLE ASKING, TALK TO GOD ON THE DAILY, I WOULD DO FOR HE AS HE WOULD DO FOR ME, WHEN THEY SAY T WE DON'T KNOW IF THEY MEAN HE OR ME, FOR A WHILE WE WERE EXCLUDED AND SEVERAL AVOIDED OUR DIABOLICAL DUALITY, LITTLE TO THEIR EFFORTS WE REINCARNATED, SEE THE SOUL BEYOND BODIES NAKED, IF IT WAS BACK THEN I WOULD BE HE WHO WAS MARTIN AND T WOULD BE MALCOLM, SINCE ITS NOW WE ARE THE VOICE OF THOSE WITH LITTLE FREEDOM AND MEGA POWER, THE ENABLERS FOR THOSE PORTRAYED AS WEEDS TO BLOSSOM AS FLOWERS, THE YING AND YANG, DUO FAR FROM A GANG, TAKE IT HOW YOU WANT, THE TRUTH REMAINS THE SAME.

THE PAIN OR THE HANGOVER?

Kanye West in his song **Dark Fantasy** asks whats worse the pain or the hangover?

shoot . . . .

the day after the previous that was full of partying, exhausting work schedules, ridiculous traffic stipulations, extended responsibilities and enhanced capabilities.

after the headache and confusions towards the resistance and solution,

I urge you to be weary of government collusion's,
see the way you step to how they want you to walk
observe how you talk in relation to what they tell you
maybe its just me who sees the hypocrisy quite possibly my mind state
perceives democracy with the eye of scrutiny and innate humility
maybe too many thoughts within your frame, only minutes after nine so most
of you dudes and gals are a sleep, unfortunate we don't think the same
imagine the power of simultaneous brains, or even friends who lived life the
same, imagine if you knew motherfuckers without even remembering a name,
animals seem to be free of official language yet immense in communication,
while they inhabit at their natural surroundings we create buildings and charge
people at prices merely astounding to see if they deserve to live in a place we
call housing
wonder what the synonym is for down sizing
see how the rebellious mind works and of what it is comprising
early in the am
perfect ass timing

<u>Synopsis</u>
I wrote this piece during one of my hangovers. I was listening to the Kanye West album - *My Beautiful Twisted Dark Fantasy*- and thought about what was worse, the pain or the hangover? I realized the pain is always worse because the hangover subsides and is usually a result of trying to drown, rid, or ignore the pain. The references in this piece indicate areas of society that cause pain to others, this is the reason for the mention of government collusions and the communication of animals. If humans could simultaneously communicate in harmony the way animals do, several of the aforementioned themes (democracy, down sizing, and pain) would be reduced or at the very least addressed adequately.

CHAPTER 3
-
FICTITIOUS REALISM

RATHER
BE
WITH
YOU

this story was inspired by the song: Rather be with you by Wale Feat J.Cole & Curren$y

She walks down the street and tells the boy on the other side -with her eyes- that he should relocate himself between *her* thighs.

To her surprise dude across the way just wanted her to smile and see what she had to say, wasn't even interested in getting play.

Homegirl was beside *her* enabling tension to arise and deceiving even more than the illusionary effect of the eyes, so was it to be or not, one cannot determine unless they are willing to determine what is - but you know she into a dude and wants to get to know him better, as he's rockin' them guess jeans and argyle sweater, she manoeuvres down the street in a smooth auburn leather, hairs soft and flowing like feathers.

So what's up with you? he asks, she smiles and says not much while trying to inhibit a laugh, he knows she's sincere and despite the opposition from her friend who stares at this young man with a glare he is focused on making it very clear that he wants to connect with this girl via his two ears, asks *her* questions of significance, what's her intoxicating fragrance, areas of importance, days of remembrance, she is taken back by such attentiveness and she alludes to the contrary of stiff.

Both smiling they vibing, friend is wilding and angry that she lonely on the solo tip and really feigning for the dick, but it won't come in abundance unless she knows she can't earn nothing from it, lets get back to the backwards love in kids to the nominal of two (get it backwards?), who have blossomed in a few minutes that have allowed time to fly or now flew.

Who would have expected that the navigational intersections would bring forth sensual and intimate connection? doesn't matter who thought it, this girl's Michael Jackson Bad, dude is on that Usher and he got it, if you can't figure out that analogy then this story will never end for you happily, I could easily caress your thoughts and tell you they lived happily ever after with kids and a family, for now I will tell you that homeboy asked this fly young lady if he could have her name and number; please, and she said gladly.

Gentleman asked about her friend and what she would do, the lady left her amigo and told her man - I'd rather be with you

<u>akhirnya</u>

gotta listen to the song to understand the context of these cognitive emissions; story relates to the tune!

I love you - all of you - bless

HOLLA

AM DRIP DROPS

thinking of the slaves and their narrative ways
ponder on pioneers and life seen through the eyes of the true in the early
years
wonder how the young pregnant teen stays strong and humble
steps of the Sun's pupils down the sidewalk, observing their surroundings,
walking through obstacles with smiles, I see that as astounding
they may try and stop your passion, but passion is derivative of the soul which
evokes inspiration
look up in the sky and tell me you are not curious
pull her close and show her how she should be held
they say life is a bitch, you may not agree, just make sure you treat her like a
lady
retro version of the future, cancer spreads in many ways, viruses are transmit-
ted over the tube, lust and it's allure, your truth and the cure, live life up until
the world spins no more

-

GREATEST ALI

Greatest Ali
Cascius inspired the masses
wine, water, whiskey, wasted, raise the glasses
jesse owens, ben johnson, d bailey, bolt, whose the fastest?
historical hierarchies and classes, disillusioned messages and
unmotivated pupils in classes
words are only symbolic of cognitions so I can be the dopest,
nicest, coolest, worstest, bestest or the badest
Masonic myths and illuminati mockeries, wack darkology practiced
by redundant asses
in a world of racism I'm the blackest
Let's sleep in the world of serenity, I'll provide the mattress
mentally, emotionally, spiritually, conceptually revoke the slave's
lashes
if one can die in the blink of an eye I will appreciate the length of
my eye lashes
Troy Dennie
Cascius inspired the masses
Greatest Ali

Synopsis

Muhammad Ali is one of the people who gave me inspiration, hope and provided insight. I always admired his ability to speak with a purpose, reach the masses, be authentic and his unparrallel confidence. Cascius Clay converted to Islam and his name became Muhammad Ali, even as Cascius he inspired the masses. Ali will forever be known as the Greatest, so I alluded to the greatest 100m dash runners, the different terms we use to acknowledge greatness and ones that have not been included in dictionaries, I mention masonic myths (do your research!) because their lies can corrupt us. Ali was never one to fall prey to societal pressures or demands, he spoke out for social injustice and humanity for all. Ali was the first person to refuse service into the US army, during the war in Vietnam, in his words : **"No, I am not going 10,000 miles to help murder kill and burn other people to simply help continue the domination of white slavemasters over dark people the world over. This is the day and age when such evil injustice must come to an end."**
—Muhammad Ali
Cascius inspired the masses; Greatest Ali

<u>*Shadows*</u>

I chase my shadow

it always evades me

I jump, I run, I leap, I fall, I trip I stumble

I notice in the dark my shadow is less persistent

my shadow shows me love

in the midst of adversity it offers assistance

versus opposition it provides resistance,

23 and counting

been with me since my existence

to everything it has been a witness

dichotomy of my personal consensus

perceptual translucent juices . . .

. . . . deuces . . . .

MITHRIDATE

Mithridate in the english language is a confection that contains an antidote to every poison (dictionary.com).

If such a specific term exists then an equally deliberate process and product must be viable. Virus attacks the nervous system, poison infiltrates our walls of security, defy immunity and define weakness, accentuate meekness, how do we wean this without evoking such meanness from those who support an evil thesis?

If your body doesn't know of a virus it can't fight it, computers can't detect it can't find it, if the mind is unaware of a virus it reduces our virtual reality to blindness, we mistake pain for kindness, the world perpetuated in sorrow how do we rewind this, if we listen and be still we learn we are all psychics, love shows no bias, the most high are the flyest, strongest the nicest, smartest the quiet, liars the sliest, wisest stay silent, hate vs. hate extenuates the minus, mentally a highness, soul redemption all invited

Meditate, eradicate, prognosticate, regulate, emanate, correlate, obliterate evils, ills and poisons; mithridate.

fly baby fly

by <u>Troy Dennie</u> on Monday, July 19, 2010 at 4:13pm

Sit and wonder, do the stars go to sleep at dawn?
I used to base my future on my sense of reality back then, is it elementary of
me to base my past on the axiom of my present? Is what I feel more
important than what I know? Or is how I feel residual of what I know? Is the
voracious wind a telepathic conduit for our emotions, does the rain wash
away our sorrows and replenish our pastures? Am I too young to be thinking
so antiquated or sophisticated? Do you have any idea how much a brotha
really loves? Can you close your eyes and imagine your heaven or infinite
place of being? How many of y'all were sleeping when this was written?
Illustrious linguistics and non fictional illusions, does it add to your
confusion?
The ones who ain't up here should come fly with me!

subtilize

smiles are enormous, embrace them
hugs are insulant, retain them
trust is volatile, attain it

to hesitate is to ignore our own **aeromancy**

babies are beautiful
children are magnificent
teenagers are exponential
adults are enduring
humans are remarkable

to discriminate is to evade humanity, regress and alienate

sun and moon, man and woman, day and night
sleep to rest, rest to wake, wake to learn, learn to live, live to love
laugh til you can't, dream til fruition, walk til you fly, listen til you're heard

"rather die enormous than live dormant" - Jay Z

CHAPTER 4
-
INTERNAL SURROUNDINGS

P.O.M.

Many men and women in multiple directions,
searching for a clearer perspective, intertwined intersections of life and it's reflections;
let us collaborate and celebrate ways to exuviate disrespect, distaste, and hate.

A flower may bloom from the lowliest valley and be the fountain of hope for all who are able to witness,
while melodic similes are dispersed through headphones and mp3's. I urge you to think with the liberty of the radicals of the seventies and enlighten others with the notions of Plato and Socrates.

The youth are the future, but we are all the present, if peace is only the result of no war then let us strive for no war as the result of peace, from the seven seas to the therapeutic breeze of the west indies, please resurrect the love and force the violence to cease.

Life is a mosaic of decisions, decisions are the eliminatory process of choices, choices are the compartmentalized factions of options, options are all about perception, perception is all about how one sees, to look only with the eyes is asinine, to look however with the soul is to redefine what we know as 'yours' and 'mine' . . . .embrace the now and stop waiting for the 'time'

keep getting' yours, I've already got mine ;)

Peace Of Mind

untitled
By Troy Dennie · Friday, June 11, 2010
vibrating to the moodless chatter
silence conversing with solitude
embracement in a discussion with gratitude
observing what is clearly present
reflective, objective, through learning one becomes eclectic

;)

by <u>Troy Dennie</u> on Monday, May 31, 2010 at 7:44am

let's get it, go for it please don't hold back

in a world with so many apparent traps we elude the opportunities and don't
know how to react

what if you could smile instantaneously?

can you imagine peace and serenity intertwined in a harmonious state, can
anyone relate?

not even thinking about how others view you, because you know you are
you, and you know you do right

please tell me if this is what it sounds like, when u with someone for six
days and it feels like one night

navigating through the perils of these times, good food, nice laughs, few sips
of wine

trust the heart, it stops beating then we stop breathing, so if it is telling you
something its for a reason

yeah I know what you thinking . . .things just never work out for me, the
road to the top is so tough

but check this out . . . .when you get to the top what else is there to do?

being congnizant is the key, soul reflection the remedy, tutotirals of that
dude: somethin somethin Dennie

Just let me know...

by <u>Troy Dennie</u> on Saturday, May 15, 2010 at 11:57am

Just let me know,
is the sunrise symbolic of growth?
Does the moon shimmer over the pond to keep the frogs
from loneliness?

Will I see all those faces that left before I could say bye
The way I'm feelin right now, is it crazy to think I can fly?

Is it imminent that the world will rejoice in love and
prosper in peace while indulging in tranquility?

Can my intellect merely be sustained, erratically subdued
or simply misconstrued?

With so much to lose, where do we gain?
Is love the ultimate combat for pain?

Do y'all even really be taking in the stuff that I be sayin???
Maybe it is all a game
Damn, just let a brotha know. . . .

<u>Synopsis</u>
This being the second last piece in the chapter : Internal Surroundings, one must ask themselves why is it placed here? Once again you should let me know and essentially let yourself know the answers to the questions placed in this piece. I speak on truths through my eyes and return them to you as questions. Life is a funny game, one of the most amusing parts of life is being able to find answers within the questions. Do y'all really be taking in the stuff that I be sayin ?
Just let me know . . .

HUMBLED

by <u>Troy Dennie</u> on Saturday, April 10, 2010 at 8:27am

As I wake up, my eyes are shocked by the magnificent source of light shining through my window.
I take a second to notice Mother Nature light up our world, I am humbled.
Proceeding to brush my teeth, shower, get dressed, encompassing all the human made devices that helped me get ready, I am humbled.
I say good morning to my parents who have raised me, came to this country with nothing but a hope and a dream; have experienced over a century of smiles, lessons and growth.
They smile at me and say I love you, once again I am humbled.
My day continues as I cruise down the streets in another miraculous device we call a car, a tap of the gas pedal and I am gone. Humans made this? The enormously tall structures devised for business meetings and condo constituents, huge malls, stores on every corner, printable texts, hand held devices, music bangin' from the speakers, mothers strolling with young ones in the stroller, senior citizens running to sustain their cardio vascular, and children playing tag in such an amusing and pleasing manner; humility is infused through me.
I step out of my car and notice a bird resting up on a branch, starring at the world through its pictorial view, I hear the most rhythmic, melodic and eccentric song. No title, no production, no composer, just the bird singing.
I stop, observe, embrace, dance, smile and say to myself shoot, now I am truly humbled.

CHAPTER 5ive

-

SECRETS OF THE WORLD YOU THOUGHT YOU ONCE KNEW

$ . . . .$ . . . .$ . .   .   .$

Perpetual Debt

By <u>Troy Dennie</u> on Monday, March 29, 2010 at 1:55am

Perpetual: adjective

continuing or enduring forever; everlasting.

Debt: noun

a liability or obligation to pay or render something, the condition of being under such an obligation

The topic of this piece is moula, money, cash, dollars, benjamins, chips, loot, green; inevitably control.

Perpetual is descriptive of something that renders no end, and debt is the state of owing something. If we live a life focused on money, then we are indulging in perpetual debt. It may seem as though having a lot of money puts you ahead of the game, contrary to belief it just allows you to allocate your debt more freely and creatively. Today the world (this term is used to reflect those who live on Earth, not the Earth itself) has brainwashed it's constituents with a general premise of making money; which is really a continuum of debt. Words are merely symbols, several times we misinterpret these symbols and misuse the words. The words debt, fee, payment, and mortgage all mean the same thing: you have to give someone else "your money". A movie theatre has a fee of $11 , its still a debt, however it is much more affordable so rather than scare away potential customers by calling it a debt, the word fee is allocated for such usage. Rogers, Geico, Lexus, all are reasons for monthly "payments", let us ponder for a minute shall we? If one did miss a 'payment' for one of the previously mentioned companies would it increase or decrease the amount of our payment? I feel it would possibly increase the dollar amount of our payment and thus creating more implications for how we tend to our payments.

It is still the same premise, to relinquish 'our' money to someone else...sounds like debt to me.

Now mortgage, this is the one that really gets us folks. the irony of the situation is comical and nevertheless quite astounding. Primarily in North America, one is expected to attend school from age 4 to 18, after which this individual is expected to pay thousands of dollars for the next couple of years in order to educate themselves. After that stage in life, the former student may have to pay off a student loan/ debt, otherwise they will start to build their life. This will consist of saving, and putting money away for other big expenditures and luxuries. One of the biggest investments will be to buy a house, after all the sacrifice one is supposed to make to get to this level, we have the next twenty or so years to pay off a mortgage/debt. I may be young, but I am fairly confident that a mortgage entails monthly 'payments' to a financial institution in order to provide temporary security of one's habitat. In reality, a lot of people end up paying off their mortgage which is really great and advantageous, then they decide to buy a cottage, "buy" is merely the verb in relation to the notion of debt.

Some of us are smart enough to save our money, as this is beneficial in a practical sense; it is simply prolonged perpetuated debt. Imminently we will have to spend that money, or the people that inherit that money will use it to "buy" something; prolonged perpetual debt.

Shoot, I have a job, I buy things, so in no way am I telling y'all to stop working and throw away your money or not to pay for things lol. I ain't that crazy. What I would like to ensure those of you who are vehemently reading this, is money should not control you or limit your decisions. Regardless of whether you have it $$$, they are going to want it. No matter how well you save, how smart you are with your money or how much you spend or make, money is designed to be used. There is no escape from perpetual debt, the money will always have a use. Do not let the money control you, it is a currency, a tool, an asset, it is not the premise of life; happiness is.

The truth is the truth, regardless of how one chooses to perceive it. Next time you pull out that twenty, or debit or credit, ask yourself when you won't have to do such to have the things you want. The answer is for you, and it will vary for all. As always, love peace, and soul.

Please

by <u>Troy Dennie</u> on Monday, March 29, 2010 at 1:35am

Please don't confuse or ridicule the verbal molecules, excuse the secular news, simply diffuse the knowledge unused and deduce the misused
Rather exquisite how humans exhibit a knack for opting to be timid within one's own shell, while him or her inhibit such limits
Opportunity comes so openly, weather derived from forces heavenly or orchestrated periodically, chances are you are where you ought to be

Choose to look deep into the soul, without fear embrace life with less perception of young and old
illuminate the heart so all thoughts lean to warm rather than cold

Why speculate , such acts accumulate hate at an irreversible rate, evil thoughts dictate the fate of those who negate serenity
With love all shall prosper, yet modern Neanderthals focus on the dollars, negligent to the dharma
let us attain infinite enlightenment, unparallel honour

REALITY

By <u>Troy Dennie</u> on Saturday, March 20, 2010 at 11:37am

A great friend of mine consistently reminds me "There is no way to happiness, happiness is the way."

We can soar as high as the mountains off the coast of Vancouver if internally we are able to emerge into the radiance of the sun and be engulfed by the sky's grace. An unaware conscience enables one to be cozened by modern day society's traps and class based info structure. An aware conscience provides one with the opportunity to embrace all of life's moments which are truly yours as well. Thoughts stem from an ever growing tree of knowledge and flow profusely as water through the Nile. As I look into the wondrous eyes of a young baby and become absolutely intrigued by the sincerity and amusement protruding from their smile, it is a time of enlightenment. The beginning of life is a struggle for survival and a sensational adventure, a time when we are concerned with what makes us happy and we have no intentions of hurting others to increase our satisfaction. We have slowly been cultivated through means of domestication, individuality is being projected through the devices we use to read and transmit messages like the one I am writing and you are reading.

Reality is reality, however reality is very relative. We have adapted to 365 day years for three out of four years, we change the time on our clocks by an hour (ahead or back) simply based on our perception of the Sun's correlation to the Earth. Reality is that the "time" does not change, what we use to manipulate the duration of life is altered temporarily; however we are still able to live our lives. My people, whom I love, please realize that if we are able to have this much control over what we perceive as time, our reality can be altered and transformed to reflect our truest and deepest dreams. Live your dream, the only difference between what we see as real and what we know as a dream is snoring. Your conscience never sleeps; your reality should never be compromised.

Holla!

imbedded in the conscience

By <u>Troy Dennie</u> on Tuesday, March 16, 2010 at 12:19am

Why choose to confuse the terms used?

Rather format plans into actions to reach intangible satisfaction. Let's engage in fruitful conversations and diplomatic relations, simplistic to aristocrat excessively inhale Mother Nature's oxygen as if it were their own. When we pass, the oxygen, the water, the wind, these undeniable elements remain; our bodies will dissemble.

Einstein said "Not everything that can be counted counts, and not everything that counts can be counted." Dually noted, referring to the aspects of life that are free from societal evaluation, yet infused to the soul.

The gut instincts and distinct urges we feel are more natural than our ability to pronounce our own names. To deny these instincts is to deny what makes us human, nevertheless suppressing our innate qualities that separate and unite us with all beings of life. With an in influx of priorities: bills, work, school, spouse, friends, homework, chilling, etc, it would appear irrelevant to focus on what is invisible to the human eye.

Interestingly enough, humans tend to complain about stress, an ailment that is not physical, and feelings of insecurity and sadness; these things are not tangible either. Point being, humans tend to complain about ish they ignore and refuse to address. The mind is a powerful tool, the soul is an empowering dynamic, our bodies our indelible reminders of our grace and potential. Look at yourself and appreciate all the features you have been blessed with in correlation to your mosaic personality, and the odds of being one in six billion because there ain't nobody like you. Individuality is prevalent in humans, hence the need for isolation. Mind, Body, Soul integration and moral stability must be imbedded in the conscience.

Quintessentially misunderstood

by <u>Troy Dennie</u> on Sunday, December 6, 2009 at 9:42am

Assumed as another from the hood, intellectual capability beyond the reach of normal

Should I apologise for my distinct views and beliefs or shall I continue to be forthright with my truth and logic

Care less about what society says than I do about how much money I should make when my family is still going to have to pay twenty to thirty thousand for my grave; hypothetically speaking.

One mind one time, no regrets, dissect the problems in life that intersect the eclectic responses to epidemics

til the whole sky is with me, and when we on the same level I illuminate my conscience, unaware of appearing as a rebel

Skin will decay, financial development does not reflect one's age, euthanasia and twelve gages are reasons for death globally, yet people worry bout ways to secrete stress, and I refuse, so I am seen as crazy. In a crazy world to be sane one must be above the crazy, so who's crazy; you feel me?

<u>Synopsis</u>

The first word of this piece tells the whole story, *assumed*. Do not make assumptions, this is how our world has become one of confusion and false messages. This is one of my older pieces yet it still holds true, quintessentially misunderstood in my eyes is being typically mistaken or misinterpreted. I feel this theme may hold true for several of us, a lot of people may know of an individual and their likes or dislikes, however to really know someone you must look beyond the surface, body, words, job, location, family; you must see the essence of the being. Last week a lady accused me of stealing a sprite from the dollar store, I had purchased it in the food court prior to entering the dollar store.

I could have responded out of malice, good thing I know that there are no bad people only dangerous decisions. A smile seemed more appropriate than tripping out on her. When it was all said and done I simply shook my head and laughed; quintessentially misunderstood.

soul expressive (pt.1)

by Troy Dennie on Monday, September 21, 2009 at 11:24pm
Evasive and ill exaggerated
Deliberated, positively correlated
Continually happy habitually
Symbolically better chronologically
Possibly a moral dichotomy
Logically the autonomy
Infinite prerequisite
Innately immaculate
Symphony in harmony
Prodigy a' Pac, Marvin, Marley

... (pt.2)

by Troy Dennie on Saturday, September 26, 2009 at 10:24pm
Ostentatious laughter
Consciously didactic
With ever glowing optimism overlapping everlasting realism
Pretentious predators
Perpendicularly positioned in my path
Shall not feel my wrath
Imperious advice
From those who disguise their vice
Supposed intentions
Unable to suffice
Invective insults
Merits incline
Compatible to false
Contemporary happiness
Within modern content
News broadcasts
The apparent relevant
External distractions
Internal complexes
Allude to my predicament

If you read this and you have nothing to *say* then cool; although if you read it you really *should*

by Troy Dennie on Monday, February 1, 2010 at 12:09am

reluctantly subdued by sleep or submerged in dormant existing, I profess the importance of living and the vitality of soul intonation this form of literature eludes conformity however is not free from feedback or scrutiny

omissive of salvation, hope and humanity, precipitating my spiritual sanctity and mental sanity, rebel with a cause and lover with flaws
disturbing talks of apocalyptical misfortunes in the near future rather redundant considering lack of ability to derail the outcome. engraved in human ignorance is the consistency to allude to the negative and be disappointed with the eventual fact
1440 minutes are given to us daily, we are so fortunate in these surroundings, many are not and constantly we are reminded of this, still only to survive by miniscule bliss; how punitive?

the money, spouse, cars, clothes, education cannot exceed or sustain the level of content that the purified soul satiates
I urge those of you who may read this to close your eyes and allow yourself to be free from fear, doubt, and ill based recognition. This is my premonition, we are all equally exquisite and a prerequisite for happiness. If you would like to be happy then smile and don't stop, we are in control of ourselves and due to media manipulation and conclusive languish of the spirit we have fallen behind and are in need of resurgence. I smile whole heartedly and love abundantly, whether it is reciprocated to the same longitude is irrelevant and beyond my control, yet my emission of serenity will not be transparent because love is a force, a power, a mind state, not a word or an act. We need to be happy, I know I am , and I truly want the same for you, soul redemption one way or the other
one love

Indeed

by <u>Troy Dennie</u> on Saturday, February 27, 2010 at 8:33am

I envision of a world of equitable humanity, free of disposition correlated financially. As Martin, Lennon and Ghandi dreamed, a place where love reigns supreme and every face is the most lovely you've ever seen. An unfathomable pedigree of compassion, residual acts of empathy, continuums of eternal bliss soaring higher than city condominiums surpassing milleniums and referendums. A world where brother and sister, father and mother, friend and neighbor, stranger and lover are replaced by the notion of one; family. In a time when guns are obsolete and no one is cognitively homeless nor sleeping on the streets. A day when religions are not at war and metaphysical interpretations deviate from segregation. Heal the world like Michael, deduce our evils and irradiate this cycle. Appreciate the teachings of life, science, music and religious doctrines like the pyramids and the bible, other beliefs rest not idle yet the core of our praises to the omnipotent internal idol. The dopest imagery without the use of similes can be painted so vividly if one closes thine eyes and embraces the heart beat. And if they ask you 'why, why?' Shoot, "tell em that it's human nature, why does he do it that why? I like lovin this way, I like livin this way." - Michael Jackson; human nature. Indeed Michael, indeed.

Smile

by <u>Troy Dennie</u> on Sunday, March 14, 2010 at 10:32pm

In this day and age we have become so blind.
The initial phase of admiration for the sensational atmosphere has eluded us. In order to grasp the concept of deeper meaning to life, one will have to forgo previous cognitive limits and embrace new fundamentals. We must refrain from complaining if we are not fit to make a change. It is unrealistic to expect the same treatment from others, give without conditions, regardless of the nature of such acts. **Humans** are exemplified through greed and suffering, the greed causes suffering and suffering always takes away before it gives back. In writing my ideologies and outlooks, I had hoped to acquire the interests of those whom I care for. Life has taught me many lessons, one of them being: you cannot expect anyone to live or look at things the same way you do. Each individual has their own choice and must fulfill their own priorities and needs. With this being said I have learned to change from hiding behind my smile to embracing my joy and deflecting the ignorance of others. Though it may seem more applicable to reiterate notions that fulminate based on erudite accumulated, I much rather dissimilate metaphysical disturbances with conscious occurrences. If reading this makes you smile it is likely due to your comprehension, hence the humor. If reading this perplexes you or imposes a feeling of being slighted, do what I do. . . . .
SMILE

03-07-2010

by Troy Dennie on Sunday, March 7, 2010 at 6:59pm

Living life to the fullest in the dopest reality

Ain't fixated on salaries or the proportion of calories.

Chilling in an abundance of love consumed by the real.

Medicinal notes anecdotal regarding the spiritual, so deep and cryptic the real mind can't miss this,

lame ones can't get with this.

Remarkable how I transform convictions previously lamented in parenthesis to the emphasis.

Ridiculous is the hypnosis.

Gelid with the mental flow, intuitive with the soul, inept to the hate, indulged in harmony enabled by the

influx of love, limited by the boundless measures of energy, exuberant with the emission, cool with the

cognitions.

Explicitly exquisite with linguistics. Strategize to super succeed my successes and successors.

Preordained preparation periodically potent. Riddles, rants and rhymes reattributed, consistent as

hypotenuse;
humble
as
Dr. Seuss

CHAPTER 6
-
USE YOUR REAL EYES
&
REALIZE

your title
by Troy Dennie on Sunday, March 21, 2010 at 11:49pm

look as if your eyes could only see temporarily

speak as if every word were your last

run like a cheetah as your limbs propel you forward

laugh like it is infectious

learn the most you can and have fun doing it

listen attentively and embrace the didactic nature

smile as much as possible, try to make others smile too

love like you can't be hurt and live knowing you can

inhale slowly exhale appreciatively, be grateful for the small things

know who you once were in order to know the new you

a fist with fingers up, no more or less than two.

PEACE

My name is Kaitlin Schoenmakers and I am a University of Toronto graduate currently continuing my studies in the social work field. I've been friends with Troy for almost ten years and I've known for a while that this book was only a matter of time. We met as thirteen year-olds in our first year of high school and now he is more like a brother. When I was asked to write about one piece I knew this would be a hard task because all of his work is so incredible. My favourite, however, is called your title. I love this one because Troy and I both do our best to live our lives with love and whenever I need reminders of how to do that, I turn to Troy. I feel as though this piece allows everyone else to see how beautiful life is if you just see it that way. Use these words to inspire; yourself, someone else, the world. I am honoured to know Troy and through this piece others get to see a little bit of him too.

ummmm ya.....
Distrait with pecuniary
Gelid visionary
Mind serenaded with blissful aubades til sunset
Life full of mistakes, journey full of lessons, debates of delegated questions with mosaic
answers
How hypocritical are the anecdotes of the biblical, we reduce truths of sikhs and islamics to
miniscule
While we are too diminutive to see from where Hinduism and Taoism are derivative
The divisibility amongst humanity is residually problematic, ever present like static the
beaurocrats, conservatives and democrats got the cheese, we all up in a maze, we the rats,
who reacts and fights BACK on terrorism of Anglo-Saxon, Caucasians - *mangaloids*,
Latinos, south east and west Asians, Jews and the black, young, the poor and needy, helpless
and the greedy, if one was upon last meal who would be righteous enough to feed the? Many
parents and theirs alike came here to live freely so we indulge in the lavish endearing seen on
TV, success may be hard but failure just to easy, so ALLAH, BUDDHA, GOD, SCIENCE,
LEBRON OR JEEZY, its the lessons not the teachings, y'all gotta believe me

synopsis
Distrait with pecuniary, I am detached from monetary ambitions. I love my life and my aim is
to live a wonderful life rather than make a living. I read the bible, in no way am I demeaning
the Bible, I am shedding light on the fact that humans wrote the Bible and there are
contradictions within the Bible. The message within the Bible is of peace, love and respect
for God, I am completely down for that. This piece is based on North America, the WE refers
to how our society operates in the Western Hemisphere. I mentioned all races and several
dispositions to encompass all, the more we embrace the oneness of life and unity of all the
closer we are to our Kingdom. Being cognizant, loving and aware is more important than the
act(s) that bring about such freedom.

AIN'T TRIPPIN'

steps to escalating levels
drops of inspiration pour from the pores of life
until you know the path you will not see the residuals
not being able to see something is contrary to it not existing
show me love if its what you feel
I show all love cuz its whats real
let the trees just chill out with you
all they wanna do is help you breathe
so I don't see no harm in feeling the breeze

tadpoles and aqua based lives peruse the most dominant force on our planet
water triples, expands and ripples
my words caress, soothe and tickle
if most put their two scents in, consider my prognostications to be products of a nickel
I know I have you speculating, affirmed or tripped out
even if it is only just a little
tell me which one of the latter day saints has comprised methods of endearing aspirations
for the youth, for today that is the riddle
pardon me as I excuse myself to abundantly giggle
I don't like to be presumptuous but I feel as though you are caught up in the middle

WHAT UP

kiss the ones close to you
remember you don't have to say yes if you
don't want to
reciprocity is the kryptonite of our economy
but it is essential to our harmony
pass others and say hi, I opt for the word
peace rather than bye
either way you look at it your boy stays
high, makes sense since I dwell in the truth
and long for the sky
not here to give up, authentic from the toes
up, on the next occasion don't say not much
because now you know whats up

Wordz

words to translate
acknowledgment of vibrations and rhythms,
we call them feelings

                Marvin believed in sexual healing,
                  the poor allude to stealing

                                      my source is infinite
                                        style exquisite
                          colloquially I am simply sick

when the roses die who cries?
                when it is time to go why ask why?

                              if you're happy appreciate
                          the essence of the moment,
                    you can be in it yet none own it

MY PRAYER

LORD HELP ME WITH MY MISSION TO LISTEN TO THY INTUITION.
I FEEL FOR SOME THE LESSON IS MISSING.
PEOPLE DON'T LOVE LIFE IN ORDER TO LIVE, SO MOST ARE
SCARED OF DYING AND UNKNOWINGLY DISMISSING THE NOTION
OF LIVING; MENTALLY IN PRISON AND OBLIVIOUS TO THE
VOLUMES OF WISDOM.
I BE KICKIN IT, DO THEY REALLY FEEL HIM?
I SEE YOU AND KNOW YOU, OPTOMETRISTS CAN'T MONITOR SUCH
VISION
LIGHTS, FEARS, AND ADMISSIONS
POSSESSIONS, OBSESSIONS,AND CONVICTIONS, AMBIGUATION,
PRONOUNCIATION, DESTINATION
SEE THE CORRELATION?
I RESPECT MY FREEDOM AND HENCE YOUR DECISION
MY LOVE IS PERPETUAL AND FOR THE GIVING
LORD HELP ME WITH MY MISSION TO LISTEN TO THY INTUTION

If Only 4 One Day

by <u>Troy Dennie</u> on Wednesday, February 10, 2010 at 11:02am

If only for one day

would we be more careful of those we claim to hate

If only for one day

could we engage in positive interaction and vitiate forming factions

If only for one day

would we be more conscious of the words we say

If only for one day

if life was this way,

would we be more attentive to the ones who stray

If only for one day

could we embrace the moment, ponder on tomorrow or reflect on yesterday

If we lived

Only for one day

Would I recognize you as someone other than one who shares the blood of my mother?

If only for one day

would I wait til night to tell you I love you

If only for one day

could we restrain from saying fuck you

If only for one day

would we do all that we said we would, and live in all the ways we could differentiate bad from good

understand the burbs and the hood, the rural and the desolate

where infinite and limits intersect, where the stream of life ends and the imminent interjects

would we be focused on lust, greed, money and sex
could we foresee the end of omitting trust, compassion, serenity, and respect

If only for one day

would those we lost return to our arms, would it be easier if they have never left our hearts?

If only for one day

would we be more careful of the bed we lay, say it is so nice to see you rather than hey,
would we still be engulfed by addictions or peacefully abide submissions

all these questions as I sit here and press play, but still I ask, what if life was

Only for one day

If Only 4 One Day Introspect...
First of all I would like to say bigups' to my brother from another mother, my other half,
Troy Dennie aka T-Nyce. I never thought I'd be here today writing an intro spec for a book
that my homie published, ya'll gotta pardon me... this feeling is simply amazing. I've seen
Troy blossom from an innocent little boy with a smile and charisma to this strong minded,
conscious thinking, living by morals and smooth talking prophet, as I would like to call him.
This book has so many thought provoking pieces that are not meant for anybody who is not
ready to think outside of the box. It also has answers to many questions one has on certain
aspects of life and if they are not ready for those answers then again, this is not for them. For
those of you who want something to revitalize your body, soul and mind, then this is most
definitely for you.
If Only 4 One Day...
I chose to talk about this piece because out of all the many great ones I read it stuck in my
head the most. Using a simple phrase to catch the reader's attention, Troy adds simplistic,
linguistic and realistic examples of everyday actions that could be or should be taken if life
were only for one day. My favourite part in the piece is when he says "If only for one day,
could we embrace the moment, ponder on tomorrow or reflect on yesterday". This hits me
because he depicts a notion that very few can do effectively. Take what's in your past to fuel
you today and make better decisions for tomorrow. I feel many will like this as their favourite
piece because of its simplicity, but more than that the meaningful message behind it.
I love you T-Nyce, sky's the limit homie.... keep doing it for the people. One love homie.

CHAPTER 7
-
A WORLD A NEW

Younique

Picture little amber, in a world where she is taught to suppress anger and several won't thank her. Imagine her learning how to conduct herself like a lady, attain grades in the eighties, let us nurture her intuition and help her learn from tumbles and falls.

Can she be as noble as raj, who is used to less and undertakes more? He whom is at the temple on the daily, tends to the care of his sisters and is upholding of values and purpose.

Is he like jaana with a silent j? Whose parents are of governmental relevance and in America's eyes would be seen as immigrants, with her social independence serving as the main importance, it appears the system will be utilized by her like an ornament.

Tell me about tyrique who is low key and discrete, rocks the most humble of sneaks and operates mellow on the streets, with ladies longing for more and girls settling for the cheek.

It is the similarity in life that makes us love and the abstract which make younique.

RULESANDRIGHTS

Inspired by Lauren Hill's poem : Motives and Thoughts.

Rules and rights
Yield for traffic and proceed through red lights
Woman weren't always seen as equal
A seemingly unfathomable number of people
Confused and dazed
Workin like slaves for what pays and not seeing the lessons in days
Rules and rights
Taxes must be paid
Laws must be obeyed
Illegal to sell cigarettes to minors but ain't illegal for minors to smoke em
Liquor and beer are admissible
Damage to the organs is critical
Their lies and schemes
To elude you of your dreams
Things ain't always as they seem
Why are our so called soldiers fighting for peace oversees
When ladies n gents is out here starving, homeless and bleeding?
How many muslims do you know who are willing to terrorize a flight, yet for some reason
the hypocrites who tell us to assimilate within society and normality are the ones to inform us
that bigotry is still alright...huh
Tell me about these rules and rights
Like right to freedom of speech
And the freedom for cops to search
Rights of birth, to be a blessing! Temporarily on earth
Rules of institutions, children's lack of rights
My thoughts escapade and ascend like my breaths in the night
Mothers workin a nine to five and servin meals at night, immigration laws enable folks to
come in the evening, authorities can have em deported at sunrise,
Their rules force you to close your eyes
You see with only your pupils and we all become dilated pupils of those with cruela devilles
for motivators, get it cruel aaa devil.. They put it in front of you, tell you what to read and
how to write, what they gotta look like to be your type, who can make you try their new
style, someone cool and fun, nice and attractive, that's the demo, you're the audience, once
your dollar signs and contentions serve as applause then they further extend their clause,
which in turn brings me to santa, why do we feel a need to marvel our children with lies and
disguise them with pronouns like fairy tales...
Rules and rights
Are we celebrating Jesus' birthday or his life?

Are the decorations commemorative of the stars and light which lead the three wise men or merely a means of bright?

In aramiac or hebrew their ain't no J so what should we call him, could we possibly allude to Christ,

And if so then is Christmas the story of his birth and hence inspiration for us and our daily vibes,

Or once again his life and if so let's never take the Christ out of Christmas and don't even mention the x cuz that ain't right

If working wasn't mandatory or perceptually necessary how would you be living your life?

Does love transcend and engulf all even more than the theme of husband and wife?

Wowsers, working for the slender pieces of paper stashed in purses and trowsers, ain't no way this is what the source, creator, mother father, God, Allah painted it like

Rules and rights

synopsis

Rules were initially designed to provide structure and guidance, now they are used as a means of control and manipulation. Rights should never be constituted by the government or Charters. We as members of life and love all have the right to peace, respect, nourishment, and shelter. If you notice, several of our brothers and sisters have to migrate to a new country in order to **feel** peace and respect, an estimated 15 000 000 children die of hunger per year; while a good fraction of us enjoy buffets, fast foods and grocery stores. Lets talk about this shelter thing, I mean if you don't have a social insurance number you can't get a job, no job no credit, no credit no house, no house you homeless, homeless aren't legally able to sleep on the streets in Canada, most homeless shelters will only let you stay for two weeks, imagine how hard it is to land a job with no home number or address. This is what many have come to know as **life**, these cotdamn rules and rights.

THIS IS

this is where the money won't matter
only positive chatter
when it comes to moving up, I am elevating on <u>Heaven</u>'s
ladder
this is where my thoughts dwell
this is where I tell you whats really good and from there
you can decipher what's cool, what's happening, what's up
and what's hood
this is where I tell my brothers and sisters that our siblings
are around us in colonies, cities, counties, villages and
nations, and they are waiting for a change, we must not
keep them waiting since they have been extensively patient
this is where I vibe to the motionless serenity of the
cemetery and embrace the counterbalance of life and see
that life and death are one in the same rather than contraries
this is where the real become illuminated and the occult are
obliterated
this is where you realize what it is like to fly and remain on
the ground
this is where we embrace the teachings of <u>Einstein</u> and
know energy is within and all around, understand that what
we perceive as matter is merely energy whose vibrations
have been reduced to the extent of our senses being able to
pick them up

this is where I reinforce the notion that our eyes can ONLY
see luminous light so you might want to focus on what the
human eye cannot detect and still respect the rest
this is where I detach myself from negative vibes and tribes
and you see I am light years ahead and beyond, far past the
theme of prime
this is where the conscious thoughts extrapolate and simplify
this is where I am whether you view Troy as dead or alive
this is where yessur; gratitude and cognizant relevance was
derived
this is where I'm at
this is where you may wonder about or quest for
this is where we are all from and this is the exemplification
of love
this is where it is, will be and always was
THIS IS

Gestures of Love

Salutations!

From the purity of my heart, I thank you for taking time in your life to read my thoughts. Secrets of a World Untold is a compilation of several pieces, and essentially is a compilation of a lot of positive influences, energies, and people. I would like to take the chance to express gratitude to all those who have been part of this process and extend a formal thank you.

Several gracious souls donated selfless gestures of support, I forever appreciate their kindness.
Thank you,

Darrell, Jackie, Katie, Carole and Hen, Trav, Court, Matt "beef", Iziah, Derek, Hasani, Genest, Michelle, Rudy, Gary, Amde, Stuart, Dave and Steph. To those I did not mention, please know you are fondly remembered.
I want to thank my boy Tony and his cousin Alex for contributing to my book artistically via photos and illustrations. See more of their work at Sessions Shop at the Brampton Flea Market.

I would like to thank my family; my mom and dad for always supporting me, fostering my freedom of expression and creative thoughts. You have listened to a plethora of my writings and poems, being able to express my cognitions to you is immensely rewarding. Love always.
My siblings: Andrea for encouraging me to publish my

work and taking my thoughts abroad, Lori Ann for always being honest with me and loving, Tamara for keeping me grounded and expanding on my thoughts, Trina for accepting nothing less than clear and concise answers from not only me but everyone, Shane for inspiring me to create my identity and solidify my quest in life. These words are just acknowledgements, our bond, communication and laughter shared evoke my fondest memories. I love you immensely

I would like to thank Nana, Max and Jods for expressing ways I can convey my message in the most feasible and humble of ways, it is much appreciated. I want to thank Nader for always listening to my pieces and being honest with feedback, nuff' love my dude. I want to thank my grandparents for fostering my positive thoughts and sheding insight on relevant world issues. Paula, thank you for all you have done and continue to do. I truly cannot tell you how appreciative I am, and how humbled I am by your support. Three!

I want to thank my closest friends who blessed me with introspect pieces for my book. Tyrone, you are my other half, my confidant, I respect your integrity, honesty and purity. Thanks for always being real with me and supportive of me, I love you infinitely homie; bless.

Kaitlin our friendship is a constant reminder that love holds no boundaries, I'm so glad that we've been able to grow together and learn so many things; a true blessing.
Emma you're ambition and zest for life are truly gifts from

God, please continue to live your life in such fashion, may this friendship never die.

Thank you to all, may love spread to each corner of the World and beyond. Dream big and live beyond your dreams, trust God, be kind to all and stay true.
Peace

Please visit www.troydennie.blogspot.com
Follow me on twitter @troydennie

Stay true, embrace the breeze, and smile unconditionally.
Love for all, conscious of one.